Animals That Help Us

Therapy Animals

by Alice Boynton

LOOK!
BOOKS™

Red Chair Press   Egremont, Massachusetts

Look! Books are produced and published by Red Chair Press:

Red Chair Press LLC   PO Box 333   South Egremont, MA 01258-0333

www.redchairpress.com

Publisher's Cataloging-In-Publication Data

Names: Boynton, Alice Benjamin

Title: Therapy animals / by Alice Boynton.

Description: Egremont, Massachusetts : Red Chair Press, [2018] | Series: Look! books : Animals that help us | Interest age level: 004-007. | Includes Now You Know fact-boxes, a glossary, and resources for additional reading. | Includes index. | Summary: "You know that pets can be fun. But some dogs, horses, pigs, and more have important jobs to do. With Animals That Help Us young readers will discover how animals help us stay safe. Some animals are especially suited as therapy animals to help people feel less stress. Readers will meet cats, dogs, rabbits and more who visit schools, hospitals, and even nursing homes to help us feel safe."--Provided by publisher.

Identifiers: ISBN 978-1-63440-314-6 (library hardcover) | ISBN 978-1-63440-362-7 (paperback) | ISBN 978-1-63440-320-7 (ebook)

Subjects: LCSH: Animals--Therapeutic use--Juvenile literature. | Animals as aids for people with disabilities--Juvenile literature. | Stress management--Juvenile literature. | CYAC: Working animals. | Stress management.

Classification: LCC RM931.A65 B69 2018 (print) | LCC RM931.A65 (ebook) | DDC 615.8/5158 [E]--dc23

LCCN 2017947556

Photo credits: Shutterstock except for the following; cover: © Spencer Grant/ Alamy; p. 5: Linda F. Radke, Story Monsters LLC; p. 7: © MBI/Alamy; p. 9: © Imagestate Media Partners Limited - Impact Photos/Alamy; p. 11: © REUTERS/Alamy; p. 13: © Jane Williams /Alamy; p. 17: © Marmaduke St. John/Alamy; p. 19: © David Grossman/Alamy; p. 21: © Emanuele Capoferri/Alamy; p.22: © Sylvie Bouchard/Alamy

Printed in the United States of America

0718 1P CGF18

Table of Contents

What is a Therapy Animal?

Meet some therapy animals. Their job is to help people with special needs. Therapy animals go to hospitals, nursing homes, and even schools. Wherever they go, they get a smile and a big hello!

A good therapy animal loves being with kids and adults.

A therapy animal must pass lots of tests. It must be friendly and **calm**. Why? It will meet many different people. Three or four people may want to pet it at the same time.

Good to Know

Unlike seeing-eye dogs, it is okay to give therapy dogs lots of attention.

Therapy Cats

Some pets can be therapy animals. Friendly cats visit nursing homes and hospitals. Petting a cat makes people feel calm. What relaxes people the most? The cat's purr!

What if a person is **allergic** to cats? No problem with a **robot** therapy cat! The robot cat is soft. Pet it, and it purrs and meows. Ahhh! The person feels so relaxed.

In 2001, a toy company in Japan invented the first robot cat. It felt just like a real cat!

11

Therapy Rabbits

Gentle rabbits are good therapy animals, too. Cuddling a rabbit makes people happy. Rabbits are just the right size for someone's lap. And their long ears and soft fur are perfect for petting.

Therapy Dogs

Here comes a therapy dog! The children in the hospital are sick. Maybe they are a little scared, too. They pet the dog and play with it. The dog cheers them up.

Good to Know

Dogs must be at least one-year-old to be a therapy dog.

Some therapy dogs go to schools and libraries. They help children become better readers. How? A child reads to a dog! The child practices his skills. The doggie buddy helps the child do his best. *Good job!*

Therapy Horses

A therapy animal can be any size—even as big as a horse! Riding a gentle horse helps people with special needs feel healthy. It makes people feel calm, too.

Good to Know

Besides being fun, riding a horse helps with balance and posture.

People who use wheelchairs can ride horses. So can people who are blind. Some people with special needs become very skillful. They win **competitions**.

Therapy animals love people.
They don't care if a person
is young or old. It doesn't
matter if someone is sick
or cannot walk. They are
happy to help.

Words to Keep

allergic: react by itching or sneezing, for example

calm: not nervous or excited

competition: a test or contest

robot: a machine that is like something real or alive

Learn More at the Library

Books (Check out these books to learn more.)

Hero Therapy Dogs by Jon M. Fishman.
Lerner Publications, 2017.

Stella: The Dog with the Big Heart by Thea Feldman.
Simon Spotlight, 2015.

Therapy Cats, Dogs, and Rabbits by Jennifer Fretland VanVoorst.
Bearport Publishing, 2013.

Web Sites (Ask an adult to show you these web sites.)

American Humane Hero Awards: Mango, the therapy dog
http://herodogawards.org/dog/mango/

Horse Therapy (YouTube)
https://www.youtube.com/watch?v=3HaXBrHCG7s

Therapy Dogs of Vermont (for reading)
https://www.youtube.com/watch?v=Rve1DukX3Mo

Index

About the Author

Alice Boynton has over 20 years of experience in the classroom. She has written many books on how to teach with nonfiction.